A Thousand Flamingos

Sanober Khan

Copyright© Sanober Khan
ISBN 978-93-85945-09-0

First Edition: 2016
Rs. 200/-

Cyberwit.net
HIG 45 Kaushambi Kunj, Kalindipuram
Allahabad - 211011 (U.P.) India
http://www.cyberwit.net
Tel: +(91) 9415091004 +(91) (532) 2552257
E-mail: info@cyberwit.net

Printed at Repro India Limited.

Contents

Wingless

My words lie wingless today
scattered about the house

no clouds envelope them today

not even the ones
bursting with a long summer evening's
luminescence

that I swore were the most beautiful
I'd ever seen

even the rain-sparkled breeze
at dawn
fail to stir them

their emptiness
stretches forever
like things said
but never done

no memories carry them
in swirls of fragrant smoke

no touches, no blushes warm
them like lotus blossoms
in the sun

they lie heavy
on the floor

without song
without substance

gathering
dusk
and dust...
and despondency

and then,
I feel You
entering my mind

like a breath
of golden beams

cascading relentlessly..
through me

releasing
my heart

and words take off
like a thousand flamingos.

Don't Mind Me

Don't mind me, my dear
if I tell you silly, strange things, at times

like I may tell you,
that black coffee sometimes, tastes like
high quality chocolate, and you
may never agree

I may tell you,
that I find the sea more beautiful
in a thunderstorm,
than on a beach-summer day

I might tell you, that the bird
perched outside, has a bit
of a schoolboy crush on me

that I have woken up... quite sloshed
from night-mingled rains,
a little drugged, by mountain fogs

that I have been kidnapped
for years....by a mere kiss

and you,
might shake your head

I may tell you...of my plans
of running away to Antarctica
in a dead serious tone

Don't mind me,
I come with a penchant
for odd behavior too

I might stop mid-evening walk,
mid-conversation... to stare
at an owl swooping down
and remain speechless
for a good chunk of time

I may continue
scraping wildly at my long-finished
cup of blueberry frozen yogurt,

some other times,
I may be itching all over
to do headstands in a crowded place

Don't mind me...just for the thrill
of a newly acquired feat

Don't mind me, if I tell you
things about life

dark things, maybe
mysterious things...

that life is nothing, sometimes
but a wound...left to heal

that the crescent moon beneath
the passing clouds, is actually

a kiss left in the sky.

All I've Yearned For

All I've ever yearned for...
are the tunes
of mountain flutes

playing
upon the lips of wind
for birds of spring

to come and flower
my backyard....like little poems
for the freshness and warmth
of a home-cooked meal

for just enough time in the world
to watch father sleeping
with folded hands
and to hear the afternoon lilt
in mother's voice

for cotton blossom kisses
of summer skies

for just enough of
good health...to go brisk walking
across a country park

for the fizz
of a shared laugh

when nothing else is
worth drinking

for the tranquility
of the moon

for my heart to be
bedewed ....with the ache
of an emerald
early morning rain
and you.

Silent Night

Let the nights come like a clearing
in the woods....with a silent
beckoning

where I may gently
become aware
of surreal moon-winds
cocooning my skin

of winter mist-spun skies
suddenly, sparkling
with revelations

of lucid dreams
sparking fantasies
and cushioning realities

the bliss of
slow dancing with sleep

of blessings
soft and forgiving
as my pillow

where darkness
is a healing balm of light

where the sapphire depth
of my own love...startles

and warms
and wounds my soul

and never really stops
deepening

engulfing the night
as a whole

where nothing else matters

where the only wonder
warmth and validation I need...
is my own.

Inseparable

May your sunlight remain
entangled in my hair

May your dust
fill the corners of my house
one that can never be swept away

May your cherry blossoms come
and unbearably sweeten my rivers
a memory that eternally serves
as sugar at teatime

May our twilights mix together
like breath and breathlessness

May our snowflakes mingle, mid-air
and hit the earth as one

In a world full of parting,
may we be eternally entwined...
like dark blue and blueberries

like bookmark and a favorite page
birds and birdsong

like water and thirst
pillow and sleep
like fragrance and skin.

Lilac Dawn

Come, my dear
suffuse my skies
with your tender light

be the tug of a distant
lavender moon
the one I can feel, even
in my deepest slumber

be the kiss in my hair
that no one sees

move...when I move
sigh...when I sigh

be that line from a poem
that I hold in my eyes
and gaze upon
my vast home of horizon

come tumbling down
with me, whenever I laugh

be my wildest ambrosia
and purest heartache

be the touch
of far off, smoky mountain winds
that I yearn to feel

scatter as a prayer
escaping my lips

as orchids
blooming in clouds

and stay, my dear
stay...

forever, as my quiet song,
in my lilac dawn.

Moonlight on my mother's face

You have probably seen

a moon
drizzling its luminous liquor
across the high
and low seas

a moon,
glowing like silver-gold fairies
through the slightly
damp leaves
of an almond tree

a moon over mountains
and hillocks
seeping into the roofs
of small, humble homes

over winter-sown
dreams and landscapes

a moon,
that sometimes
looks like a mellowed sun

pale and bloodless
by noon

a moon,
that rests in the quiet corners
of a lover's lips

you might have danced
in a moon-rain, too

But, my friend
have you ever seen

a moon

shining

over another moon?

All my life

All my life
I have looked for poems
to elope with.

End of the day

At the end
of the day

all we
ever need

is something

that helped
pass the time

and something
that keeps
time from passing.

Restore

All the colors
have started
to drain from the sky

the apple-trees
have lost their blossoms

the summer seas
no longer sing
their warm shoulder-lilt

precious things seem to be lost

what once belonged
seems abandoned

But the time will come, my dear
when I will hold you close

and all will be
right again
in the world

rivers will find
their lost course
the wilted will bloom
empires will be restored
and all the distances will close

the moon will
swan down once again
lost ships will sail home

barren words
will replenish themselves

and the winds will blow
through the pine-woods

nourishing the air
with the most divine fragrance

and we will find ourselves
in the perfect balance

that we were
always meant for

with our hearts
and gazes
drifting out over
the vast mountain skies.

Rage

My dear,
we are all made of water.
it's okay to rage. sometimes
it's okay to rest. to recede.

Longings

Longings,

be soft

when you come

like the touch of a golden moon
fluttering in a delicious
rain-breeze

come like the glimmer
of distant ships...dotting the horizon
with star-kisses

come like the first sip
of a mountain-scented tea
on lonely
autumn evenings

come like a blanket
tenderly touching
my fevered brow

be beautiful

like memories
and mist
rising off a forest river

like poems blooming
in fields of silence

come and drench me
in a moment of
a deep breath
a deep love...

and fill my heart
the way birdsong fills
the trees at dawn.

It Is You

I know it is You
even before You reveal Yourself

when dawn comes creeping
out of a misty darkness
and my heart fills
with the songs
of strange birds

I know it is You
a moment of peace
that saves me
in the middle
of a chaotic day

it is You
in the wildfires
that blaze like wrath
across lands and lives

but I also know
it is You
in the tenderness
of the young, morning rain

it is You I meet
even when You hide Yourself

in the autumn moon
behind the mountains

in the childlike laughter
of my father

and sometimes in the fragrance
between beautiful words

it is You I discover
in the last thirds of the night
listening to all my worries
pour out of my eyes

an intimacy
that only the angels know about

I know You have smiled
when the peacocks dance
in full plume

and the tulip fields
sing in full bloom

when my heart
suddenly softens

in the midst of anger
and bitterness

I long
to talk to You

and then I know
it is already You
who has been whispering
in my ear all along.

A Soft Rain

In a rain so soft
and ethereal and mist-petaled
such as this

you could blanket
a baby in it, you could bathe
an injured bird,
and grasp a peach
without ever bruising it

you could sing a song
with it, making the handsomest
man fall in love
or kiss someone's forehead
without ever disturbing
their sleep

you could make
a new best friend with it
cozy up a home, and wipe away
somebody's tears with it

you could revive ...
a dead flower
end wars
bridge distances, and rebuild
cities and empires with it

you could heal...an old wound,
permanently

touch a soul
and coax...a long-forgotten
a long treaded-over dream
back to life with it

a rain like melting pillows...

a rain so beautiful
I could never
have let go of

if not certain
that someday...it would find its way
into my poem.

Tangible

Who says poetry
is not tangible...

I, for one, have rested
my drowsy head...upon its
moon-versed pillow

I have pressed its warm hand
against the winter
of my cheeks, I have walked

beside it, too, its presence like a secret
song in my hair, in the middle
of a crowded street

have tasted it in whipped
butterscotch of clouds

felt it bubble over the
tiny glass of my own
happy laugh

I have played with its dangling
crystal earrings of rain
lit by a 5 pm sun

I have sat down...beside it
gazing wistfully out at the
ageing sea

used its rare essence
to flavor my tea...and my temper
my touches... my kisses...

waved its magic wand
to stop time in its tracks
and carried it around
like riches in my pocket

I have waltzed, and whirled,
swum from heaven to heaven
floated in and out of my body

been kissed...full
on my soul's lips
all the while sitting,

in a coffee shop, amid
unsuspecting strangers.

Warm Bird

Sometimes I like to caress
love, like a small bird
between my hands

nuzzling the warmth
of its life... against my own
marveling at how fragile
yet fierce.. it can be

knowing it will always
belong to me, but cannot
always be with me

for we all have
our own twilights and mists
abysses, to return to

realizing love must leave
behind, much to cherish
and much to mourn

knowing that love can
embellish its beginning
and sing its blossoming
and leave eternities behind

but never.....explain its loss

its grief

for how...why must it all
come to be
from the sweetest nectar,
to a tasteless cup of tea.

Bloom

This life
has been
a landscape
of pain

and still,
flowers
bloom in it.

You Have Begun

You have begun to sink
so deep
into my life

trickling into
every inch and pore

seeping like the scent
of an over-flowery detergent
into my clothes

that you seem to be present
in every squirt, of my shampoo
and sip of black coffee
every clang of my spoon,
and the shuffle of my heels,

long settled like dust
behind photo frames

that if I attempted
to clean, scrub
and vacuum my home

You'd still be...
in the cracks, and crevices
in the nooks and crannies
like invisible residues

that if I began to draw
myself away from you,

We'd still be like
two mixed colors of paint
impossible to separate

and if I stopped
writing about you
you'd still be
in the blank pages,

for what was never
written,
cannot be erased

you have sunken
so very deep into me

that if my soul were to be
wrung out,
like a piece of
rain-soaked cloth

you,
and you alone,
would ooze out of me.

Thoughts

How is it that
You are always
in my thoughts

Even when
I am not
thinking.

Blessings

May the mornings come
like a gossamer curtain...billowing
with murmurs of rain breeze
chocolate-flavored coffee
and poetry hangovers...

May the afternoons lull over
like the fisherman's boat
upon an idly gleaming
golden-tipped
grey sea

May the evenings echo
like a father's resonant laugh
with a heart unburdening
and reaching out
to another's

May the nights always be aglow
with the bliss of the day
with unharmed hands and feet
and kissed cheeks

With a calmed-down soul
star-fulls of breaths, and pillows
with a moon streaming down
in nourishing light

With gliding owls, under skies
scented with chamomile teas
magnolia trees
and holy silences.

A Poem in the heart

A poem in the heart is worth
more than a million dollars
in the bank account

a single poem, alone
can turn tides
scatter galaxies
and burst forth with rivers
from paradise

a poem in the heart
the equivalent of the purest
honeys, and finest cashmere
the steeliest armor
and the most tender kiss

an entire year's
celebrations and festivities

a single poem,
worth a hundred
cozy winter nights
kind words
and healed wounds

a single poem...
the highest peak on Mount Life

a single poem
the thing that can keep me...
light on my feet,
when my soul is
heavy with sorrow.

Vanish

Moonlight disappears down the hills
Mountains vanish into fog
and I vanish into poetry.

Rain-Swept

(tribute to my missing pet pigeon)

These days the afternoons come adorned
with a bouquet of fresh rain

with solitude hanging
in huge, grey
coffee-cups of clouds

You can see the sun, too, sometimes
dusting the waves
with golden mist

permeating the air
with a special kind of gloom,

No one can feel this pain
the way I do

I share this moment of wonder
with a wild pigeon
who lifts one thirsty wing
to the sky

and feel a sharp longing
to caress it in my hands

Sometimes I don't know, which moment
which cool gust of wind will come

and enchant me
tousling my hair
and my heart

stirring...that familiar ache of poetry

which drop will kiss
that old wrench in my soul
reminding me, all over again

I miss you better in the rain.

Acceptence

I had embraced you...
long before I hugged you.

Beautiful

You must come
and see me again, my dear

right after I have read
a new poem

Watch, how the sun
slowly rises
from behind my ear

new lines, new countries
spring up in my palms

my rough hair
becomes swaying silk

and all the leaves
in my body
become lusher than fruits

all the splendors
of the universe
stream out of my eyes

even my watery
shadow
becomes warm
luminous gold

if you look closely,
Words
like mysterious mermaids

come and live permanently
in the soft sweeps
and scars of my skin

I am no more
the same person
you saw
only a while ago

My dear
Can you not tell?

I have become more beautiful.

Sometimes

Sometimes
the things that make you cry
are more beautiful
than the things
that make you laugh.

A moonless night

There are moments
in the dead of night

when my eyes
go searching for the moon

over the warm
tremble of waves

then I remember

there is no moon

and I must cast
my own light
upon the sea.

Quench

Drink in the moon
as though
you might die
of thirst.

Some Words

Some words
Bring warmth
Just by being
Next to each other.

Vulnerable

Poems are fragile
vulnerable things

hold them gently
when you do

they have more blood
in them
than a heart

more bones
they walk barefoot

they cannot
afford luxury

and can
sometimes be
more sensitive
than water

they can get
sleepless too

and become
the loneliest
thing in the universe

grip them too tightly
and they begin
to lose
all their nectar
and magic

grip them
even further
and they

cease
to
exist.

Failures

The splendid thing
about falling apart
silently...
is that
you can start over
as many times
as you like.

Let your gaze

Let your gaze sweep...
across the world
like golden glazed beams, rising
with the mountain sun

mixing with rare
February rains
stirring dull aches

evoking sighs...
upon calm lips of afternoons

disturbing constellations
of winter skies

blanketing,
dark blue winds

Let it swing
across the wild
an insatiable lust for adventure
love, and miracles

Brushing against
all things bewitched

Let it stain
a thousand cheeks pink
Set aflutter
a hurricane in hearts

Let it skim
over beautiful faces, spring blossoms
and open seas

but stop....breathless
upon me.

Evening Tea

Tea is just an excuse.
I am drinking this sunset.
this evening.
and you.

An Ache

There is an ache
sometimes
sweet as lychee-blossoms
too tender
to be molded in words
too raw, sometimes

too beautiful

of a heart swollen with love
of old passions awakening,

of fears...unfathomable

of snowy lights
and stinging winds
of distant ships, and nights
glimmering with moon-waters

of friendships drawn
and dispersed...

of gazes smoldering,
and sunsets changing

of time...slipping too fast

of Decembers dissolving
always dissolving...
before my ever-dreaming
ever-wistful eyes.

Mountain Stream

My love
for you
will always be
like a mountain stream.

quiet.
persistent.
continuous.

Mystical Traveler

Let the moon come like a mystical
traveler, from halfway
across the sky

seeking shelter, right before
my window

from where it may
gently knock
upon the door of my eyes

when I'm not sure... if I'm awake
in a dream
or deeply awake

sneaking up on my one arm
that's almost...always peeking
out of my blanket
in the guise of
November's chill

evoking a longing
for mysteries...
and the mystery
of longing

dipping lower and lower
toward the horizon

from a stained, smoky yellow
to burnt-orange

to a swallowing crimson

inching closer...until our gazes
meet at point-blank,

only just beginning
to deepen

further ...
and further
like a kiss.

Strawberry

Your gaze
across
my cheeks

turned them
into
strawberry fields.

Spill the moon

You should be more careful
when you move, my dear

what with you...
spilling moonlight
into my poem, with a mere
flick of your hand

ruffling
the beehive
of my thoughts
with just one careless
lazy gaze

your smile...splitting the skies
into a million golden, grey
and turquoise verses

with your hair in the breeze
always leaving me scattered...
all over the place
in dewy-dreamed
peony-cheeked
poetry-drops of you.

A Story

I immerse
myself
in you

like
I immerse myself
into a
beautiful story.

Ravish

Before you think about
romancing me, my dear

you must first
romance my poems

come,
meet the sparkling glint
in my poem's eye

let your eyes drift over
the slow, pink heat
building
over my poem's skin

run your fingers
through its dark curls
untangling meanings

take its hand
and wear it
upon your own

each syllable
each silence
each melody
each tremble

lean in to kiss
all the places
where the ache is
the most special

then, with all the burning
tenderness
left in the universe
begin to,

undress my words.

Something mystical

There is
something
mystically
sad
and beautiful
about
how
I will
never
see you
again

but
meet you
again
and again

in poetry.

I write

I write
because
there are things in me
that cannot die.

This pain

It is a lot
of weight
to carry around
my dear,

this pain
of missing you

some days
I can wash it down
with a cup
of strong
black coffee

I can warm it
next to the
lemon tree pots
in my balcony

I can take it
for long, salty strolls
by the sea

let it dissolve
into the bones
of a favorite song

I can let it
graze

like hungry sheep
on vast green
pastures of poetry

but sometimes
my dear, it all
gets too much

and there is
nothing
I can do

but let my head
drop low
and my heart
weep skyward.

Spare Heart

Sometimes I think,
I need a spare heart to feel
all the things I feel.

Free

Holding
the evening
tremblingly close
to me

I weep
into
the sun

letting
the burden
of hope
lift off my chest

I realize

this is what
it means
to be free.

Breathe

May your love for me be
like
the scent of the evening sea

drifting in
through a quiet window

so I do not have to run
or chase or fall
... to feel you

all I have to do
is
breathe.

To be a poet

To be a poet means
to live
with a permanent wound

forever
susceptible
to either

the shade
of the sky

or someone's eyes.

Poet's Romance

You ask
if I will write a poem

I could,
I suppose

write
the most
splendiferous
one of all

but not
right
now
not when

your hands
are brewing
warm
cinnamon tea
across my skin

not when I'm
trying
to imagine
what
might happen
if you began
flowering

kisses
upon
me

My dear,
how can
I write
a poem
when I'm already
inside one?

Parallel Universe

Somewhere in a parallel universe
I have never parted ways
with the pearlescent ghost
of the moon, I have never

let the sun...slip away either
its golden sagas ... permanently
etched onto my horizon

the tang of salt never leaves
the swirling air… and the coconut trees
never stop dancing, to the songs
of breaking waves

I have never...let those sea-winged
summer evenings, melt
away from me nor ever
turned my cheeks away
from the pecks of June's rain

familiar faces are still
gathered...somewhere
around a bonfire, where garlic bread
and grilled chicken are sprinkled
with lemony laughter

I have never...bid farewell
to those lemons, or laughter,

never let the drum of adulthood
drown out the jungle stories
father told me as a child

somewhere...a small bird

still lies clasped between
my hands, in silent healing

and mother is still smiling
beside me, at a brown hen
nuzzling all of her chickens,
under her wings

and somewhere…in another
far off… parallel universe

that no one knows,

I have never been able to
take my eyes off you.

What Can I say

My dear, what can I say
I have dreamed of watching
volcanoes erupt with you
with our hands
cupped over our hearts

of sharing serene silences
like a kiss between souls
laden with peach-blossoms
and an occasional, precious stir of poetry

of drowning in silver dew
with you

of gazing over holy lands
breathing in fragrant soils

and leaning against you
when the pain of amazement
gets too much

of evenings and cups of tea shared
like words fully absorbed

and now you've left me
and gone

my mountains crumble to dust,
silences scrape like bare branches

there is nothing to drown in
but myself

no sights left to behold
only ashes to breathe in

none but my own shadow
to fold into

My dear, I have nothing to say,
my heart burns like the evening sky.

Defenses

In the end
it is words
poetry
sunsets
someone's deep blue
silk voice
mountain scents
someone's smile
eyes. that we have
no defenses against.

Fall in Love

Fall in love
with the energy
of the mornings

Trace your fingers
along the lull
of the afternoons

Take the spirit
of the evenings
in your arms
kiss it deeply

and then
slow dance
with the tranquility
of the nights.

Love me

Love me like a plum tree
in full bloom
bursting against a cloudless
crystal-blue sky

love me like tender mist
descending over
an endless
rugged mountain road

love me...with all the abandon
of a sudden wild rain

with all the mysteriousness
of deep midnight
forest echoes

love me like tears
glistening on cheeks

love me
in all my seasons
in all my phases

with all the wholeness
of light in the heart

with all the rights
and all the wrongs

but love me, especially
when life
tears me apart
and I am living in half

love me
with all the fullness
of a moon
a flower...
a breath...
a kiss.

All the words

All the words
all the poems
know
my warm, soft spots.

The only one

You are ever the only one
I want to share
a cup of moonlight with

the only one I want to be
cured by
when poetry
catches
a fever in my skin

the only one I want to
wake up inside

be caught by with flowers
sprouting
in the back of my neck

touch mountain lights with,
dissolve through the mists

the only one I want taking
evening walks in my hair

the only one I want to
gush to about
a majestic owl I once saw
gliding above me

the only one
I ever

want to give
all the peaches in my heart to

the only one
by whom
I want them bruised.

Soft fur

Poems are soft kitten furs
smoothing out
the rough edges of my world.

Gentle

Whatever you do
be gentle with yourself

you don't just live

in this world

or your home

or your skin

you also live

in someone's eyes.

Afterglow

In the afterglow
of an evening rain

I lay down
in the grass
and think of you

my body aches
like an after-kiss

breaking in soft fires
and wildflowers

My dear,
I will always be
this tender for you.

Tenderest Love

With callused hands
I tasted
the softness
of the moon

in the coldest
winds I discovered
my soul's
warmest fireplace

in the roughness
of his stubble
the tenderest love.

Oceans

She's got
oceans
tucked away
in her hair

poems swim
under her skin.

Let my heart

Let my heart know just this-

the warmth of an evening
cup of green tea

the joy
of kittens snuggling
and father chuckling

the blessing of blankets
butter cookies
and budding
love stories

the call of wild birds
in the twilight dawn

the sting
of salty tides
and beautiful words

the lushness
of longing

the pain
of tenderness

and the deep...

anguish of beauty

like dreams lifting
in an early morning fog.

Tuck the Night

At night when the world is
just about hovering
on the brink of sleep

I shall gather all the trees
and the stones, and their sagas

the stars
and their legends

all of the birds
and their secret songs

the early-spring blossoms.
their sisters and cousins

the sounds of the sea
and all of its echoes

scooping them all up...
in my arms

the winds
that ran through
the mane of the meadow horses
and all of its adventures....

the jingle
of mom's bracelets

and the roar
of father's laughter

all the butterflies
and their kingdoms
the milky skies
and their hidden dynasties

tucking them all in
under my blanket

and savor...
the wondrous
all-enveloping feeling
of safety
and contentment

with the sigh of a
pilgrim's soul
and a mother's heart.

The Prophet's Mosque

**(tribute to the Masjid-Al-Nabawi Mosque
In Medina, Saudi Arabia)**

It is where the cool marbles
flow endlessly

where a touch of sujood*
on its hard floors,
feels softer than
the most sumptuous
cotton-fur

where a moment spent
in remembrance
of Him, runs vaster
and deeper...
than the oceans in the sky

where a walk
under its midday sun
is better than resting
in the shade
of another place

a single glance
cast in the direction
of its domes,
is sweeter than
the sweetest
mountain honey

where minarets
reach like precious fountains
into the sky

where the air is
golden with serenity
even amidst
a thick swarm
of people

where the pillars
beat luminous

reflecting the evening
beams of light
that appear to be
sending salutations

where every prayer
purifies my heart
and blesses my soul

even when
it lacks words

where a single moment
of heartache
is better
than a hundred years
of healing.

(Sujood*- The act of bowing down in worship.
The hands, knees and forehead touch the ground.)